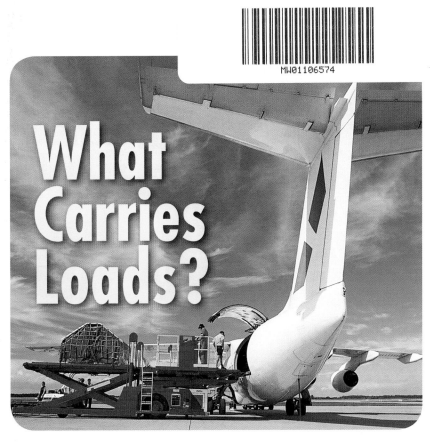

What Carries Loads?

By Katie Berk

Scott Foresman
is an imprint of

Glenview, Illinois • Boston, Massachusetts • Chandler, Arizona •
Upper Saddle River, New Jersey

Trucks carry loads.

Trains carry loads.

Planes carry loads.

Ships carry loads.

Sleds carry loads.

Bikes carry loads.

Wagons carry loads.